Test 1 (Lessons 1-5)

1 Look at the chart and write questions and answers about Rob

> *Name:* Robert Stewart
> *Age:* 16
> *Home town:* Glasgow
> *School:* Glasgow High School
> *Next examination:* GCSE
> *Hobbies and interests:* playing football and going to the cinema
> *Someone he admires:* Ian Rush

What / be / name?

What's his name.? . . . .

His name's Robert Stewart. . . . .

1 How old / be?

. . . .

. . . .

2 Where / live?

. . . .

. . . .

3 Where / go / school?

. . . .

. . . .

4 What / next / examination?

. . . .

. . . .

5 What / like / do / free time?

. . . .

. . . .

6 Who/ be / someone / admire?

. . . .

. . . .

Score:
12

2 Write offers.

(It's cold in here.) (window) . . *Shall I close the window.?* . . . .

1 (It's hot in here.) (window) . . . .

2 (I'm hungry.) (some sandwiches) . . . .

3 (I'm thirsty.) (some tea) . . . .

1

4 (It's very noisy in here.) (the TV) . . . .

5 (It's very quiet in here.) (the radio) . . . .

3 Complete the dialogue with the phrases below.

Shall I carry it for you?   Where are you going
How are you?   needn't bother.
Yes, I'm leaving in a few minutes. I can
I'll send you a postcard.   's taking me to the station.

SUE: Hi, John.

JOHN: Hi, Sue. How are you?. . . . .

SUE: Fine, thanks.

JOHN: (1) . . . . with those heavy suitcases?

SUE: I'm going to Grenada to see Natalie.

JOHN: What, now?

SUE: (2) . . . .

JOHN: That big suitcase looks very heavy.

       (3) . . . .

SUE: Thanks John, but you (4) . . . .

       (5) . . . . carry it to the gate and

       Dad (6) . . . .

JOHN: All right. Oh, here's your Dad now. Have a good trip!

SUE: Thanks very much. Bye! (7) . . . .

4 Circle the correct answer.

TONY: (a) Have you ever been b) Did you ever go to America?

ANN: (1) Yes, I a) have. b) did.

TONY: (2) When a) have you been? b) did you go?

ANN: (3) a) I have been b) I went in 1987.

TONY: (4) a) Did you b) Were you like it?

ANN: (5) Yes, it a) has been b) was great!

TONY: (6) What a) have you done b) did you do there?

ANN: (7) a) I went b) I was going to New York and Boston, and Disneyworld in Florida.

TONY: (8) What a) did b) was Disneyworld like?

ANN: (9) It a) did b) was fantastic!

Score:
9

5 Write the phrases in the correct box: *for* or *since*.

1986	yesterday	three days
Friday	twenty minutes	half an hour
last week	February	a long time

For	**Since**
three days	1986

Score:
7

3

6 Look at the chart about Susan Prince and write about her.

Age: 17
Home town: Oxford
School: Oxford High School
Next examination: GCSE
Hobbies and interests: Playing tennis and reading
Someone she admires: Chris Evert
Foreign travel: France and Germany
When: 1986
How: Train and hovercraft
Opinion: Fantastic!

....

....

....

....

....

....

....

....

....

....

Score:	
	10

Score:	
	50

Test 2 (Lessons 6 -10)

1 Look at the pictures and write sentences using *just* or *yet*.

  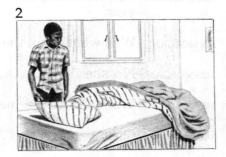

(homework) ..*She hasn't finished her homework yet.*...........................

1 (station) ....

2 (bed) ....

3 (breakfast) ....

4 (the film) ....

5 (the washing up) ....

| Score: |
| 5 |

2 Complete the conversation using *already*. Mr and Mrs Morgan are discussing Lucy's birthday.

MRS MORGAN: I really don't know what to do for Lucy's birthday.

MR MORGAN: We could take her to the zoo.

MRS MORGAN: Yes, we could, but she 's already been . . . . . (be) to the zoo. We took her last year.

MR MORGAN: Well what about the cinema? We could go to Ghostbusters IV.

MRS MORGAN: No, she (1) . . . . (see) it with Kate.

MR MORGAN: We could have some of her friends to tea.

MRS MORGAN: She (2) . . . . (have) some friends to tea. They came last week.

MR MORGAN: Isn't the circus in town this week? We could go to that.

MRS MORGAN: She (3) . . . . (be) to the circus. Andy took her on Tuesday.

MR MORGAN: Let's just buy her a nice present - a new video game, perhaps.

MRS MORGAN: She (4) . . . . (get) enough video games.

MR MORGAN: I give up! Why don't we ask her what she wants to do?

MRS MORGAN: I (5) . . . . (ask) her, but she doesn't know!

Score: 5

3 Write the past tense of the verbs to complete the crossword.

DOWN
1 ask
2 continue
3 say
7 begin

ACROSS
4 speak
5 talk
6 answer
8 reply

Score: 7

6

4 Look at the road map and complete the directions for somebody to go from Bishop's Stortford to Burwell.

B1103

Newmarket

Burwell

A45

A45

A11

M11   Bishop's Stortford

10   9

From Bishop's Stortford . . **take** . . . the (1) . . . . motorway and (2) . . . . at

Exit 9. Drive (3) . . . . the (4) . . . . until you (5) . . . . the A45. Turn

(6) . . . . down the A45 until you (7) . . . . the B1103. (8) . . . . down

the B1103 and drive down the road for about a mile.

Score:

8

5 Compare the sports, using *much*.

windsurfing / walking (fast)

. *Windsurfing's much faster than walking.* . . . .

1 windsurfing / gliding (dangerous)

. . . .

2 gliding / windsurfing (fast)

. . . .

3 ballooning / gliding (expensive)

. . . .

4 skiing / walking (difficult)

. . . .

5 hang-gliding / swimming (exciting)

. . . .

6 swimming / sailing (slow)

Score:

6

. . . .

6 Read the passage and answer True (T) or False (F).

Skiing is a much more popular sport for British people now than it was in the past. Thirty years ago, only British people with a lot of money could go skiing. There weren't any ski slopes in Britain so people had to travel to Switzerland or Austria if they wanted to ski. People didn't usually fly, so the journey, by train and boat, took much longer than it does today. It was also more expensive.

Nowadays, the journey is much cheaper and quicker. Skiers can fly to France, Switzerland, Austria or Italy in very little time. If they don't want to leave Britain, skiers can go to Scotland, where the ski industry has grown very quickly since it began in the early 1960s.

Many people who try skiing are frightened at first, because they think it is dangerous, but they soon find that skiing is much more exciting than a lot of other sports. Coming down a mountain fast gives them a terrific sense of freedom.

Skiing was more popular in Britain in the past. . .F. . . . .

1 Thirty years ago, people needed a lot of money to go skiing . . . .

2 They usually went to Scotland . . . .

3 People travelled to Switzerland and Austria by train and boat . . . .

4 The journey was slower than it is today . . . .

5 It was cheaper than it is now . . . .

6 Nowadays, people can travel by plane to France, Switzerland, Austria or Italy. . . . .

7 The Scottish ski industry began ten years ago. . . . .

8 Beginners often think that skiing is safe. . . . .

9 A lot of other sports are much more exciting than skiing. . . . .

Score:
9

7 Now write about a sport which interests you.

. . . .

. . . .

. . . .

. . . .

. . . .

. . . .

. . . .

Score:
10

. . . .

Score:
50

. . . .

Test 3 (Lesson 11-15)

1 Look at the pictures and write what happened.

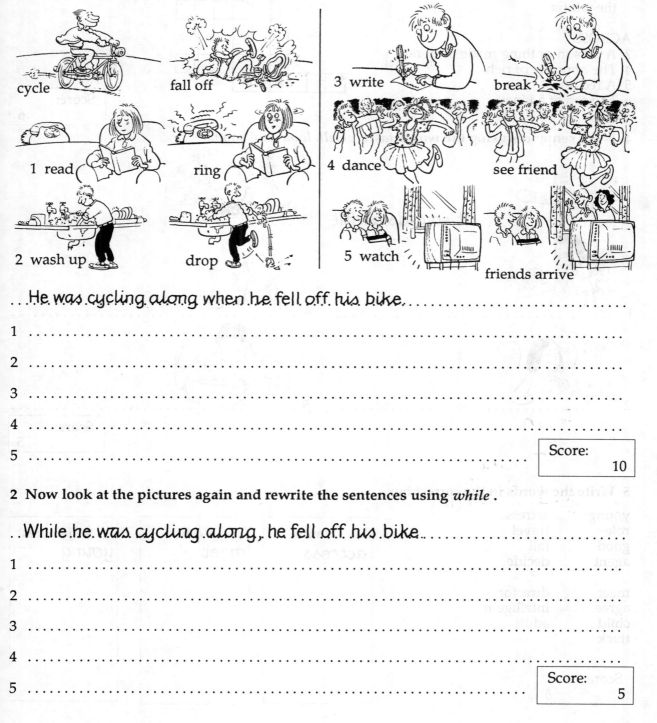

cycle — fall off

1 read — ring

2 wash up — drop

3 write — break

4 dance — see friend

5 watch — friends arrive

...He was cycling along when he fell off his bike.....................................

1 ....

2 ....

3 ....

4 ....

5 ....

Score: 10

2 Now look at the pictures again and rewrite the sentences using *while* .

..While he was cycling along, he fell off his bike........................

1 ....

2 ....

3 ....

4 ....

5 ....

Score: 5

3 Complete the crossword.

DOWN
1 The colour of gold
2 A blue jewel
3 A bird which flies south for
   the winter

ACROSS
2 A person or thing made of stone
4 The opposite of rich
5 A red jewel
6 The son of a king

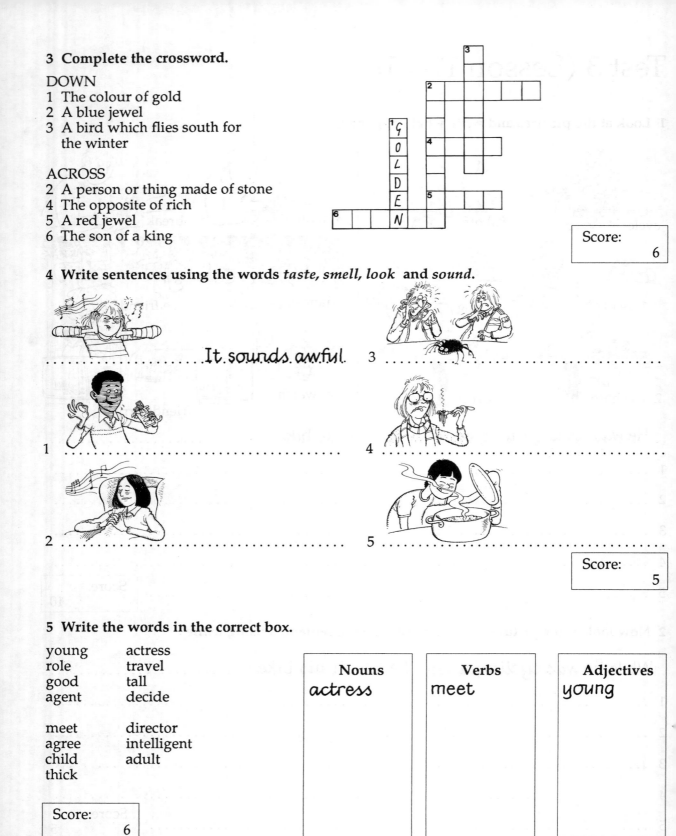

Score:
6

4 Write sentences using the words *taste, smell, look* and *sound*.

It sounds awful.

3 ....

1 ....

4 ....

2 ....

5 ....

Score:
5

5 Write the words in the correct box.

young   actress
role   travel
good   tall
agent   decide

meet   director
agree   intelligent
child   adult
thick

Score:
6

Nouns	Verbs	Adjectives
actress	meet	young

6 Complete the text with the correct form of the verb.

One evening last year, I . . .*was driving*. . . . (drive) back from work when I

(1) . . . . (have) a strange experience. It (2) . . . . (get)

dark and it (3) . . . . (be) quite late. As I (4) . . . . (turn)

a corner, I suddenly (5) . . . . (see) the lights of a car coming towards me on

my side of the road. I (6) . . . . (try) to turn my car but the other car's lights

(7) . . . . (move) at the same time. At the last moment,

I (8) . . . . (turn) the wheel of my car again and the lights disappeared. I still

don't know if I saw a ghost that night or if all I saw was the lights of my own car reflected in

the window of a shop.

Score:
8

7 Now write a strange story or adventure which happened to you.

. . . .

. . . .

. . . .

. . . .

. . . .

. . . .

. . . .

. . . .

. . . .

. . . .

Score:
10

Score:
50

Test 4 (Lessons 16 -20)

1 Complete the sentences with the correct question tag.

You're English, *aren't you?*

1 You aren't American, ...

2 You want a double room, ...

3 Andy is staying for three nights, ...

4 You don't like milk, ...

5 Andy likes milk, ...

6 They've told you, ...

7 We were only joking, ...

8 She wasn't late, ...

Score: 8

2 Write about people's preferences.

Marion ✓ film ✖ play.

Marion would rather watch a film than a play.

1 Joan ✓ fruit ✖ sweets

. . . .

2 Rob ✓ football ✖ basketball

. . . .

3 Sue and Kate ✓ disco ✖ cinema

. . . .

4 Mr and Mrs Morgan ✓ books ✖ newspapers

. . . .

5 John ✓ cycling ✖ swimming

. . . .

6 Andy ✓ fruit juice ✖ milk

. . . .

7 Mr Green ✓ train ✖ car

. . . .

Score: 7

3 Match the sentences and then rewrite them using _although_ or _however_. Write at least two sentences with _although_ and two with _however_.

Dolphins can live in the wild for thirty years. | They are in fact very intelligent.

1 Scientists think that captive dolphins aren't happy. | People still like watching dolphin shows.

2 Many people think that dolphins are fish. | In the wild they can live for thirty-five years.

3 Killer whales are called "killers of the sea". | They are mammals.

4 Dolphins in dolphin shows perform easy tricks. | They don't usually attack human beings.

5 Killer whales in captivity often die after three years. | In captivity, most die before they are twelve.

. Dolphins. can .live. in. the. wild. for. thirty. years. . . . .
. However,. in .captivity. most. die. before. they. are. twelve. . . . .
. OR .. Although. dolphins. can. live. in. the. wild. for. thirty. years, ...
. in .captivity. most. die. before. they. are. twelve. . . . .

1 . . . .
. . . .

2 . . . .
. . . .

3 . . . .
. . . .

4 . . . .
. . . .

5 . . . .
. . . .

Score:
15

4 Read the passage and answer the questions.

Kate normally watches television every day. She generally watches from seven until nine o'clock in the evening after she has done her homework. At the weekend she watches more - sometimes four hours a night. She quite likes comedy programmes but she prefers soap operas. Her favourite programmes are nature programmes, particularly programmes about African wild life. On the other hand, she thinks sports programmes are very boring. She'd rather go to bed than watch football! Kate's mother thinks that she watches too much television but in fact some of her friends watch much more than Kate. One of Kate's friends watches thirty hours a week.

Does Kate watch television every day?

Yes, she does. . . . .

1 How many hours does she watch on a weekday?

. . . .

2 How many hours does she sometimes watch at the weekend?

. . . .

3 What kind of programmes does she like most?

. . . .

4 What kind of programmes doesn't she like?

. . . .

5 Does Kate watch more television than her friends?

. . . .

Score:
10

6 **Now write about how much television you watch and which programmes you like and don't like.**

. . . .

. . . .

. . . .

. . . .

Score:
10

. . . .

Score:
50

Test 5 (Lessons 21-25)

1 Complete the conversation using *may, will, 'll* or *won't*.

DENTIST: Open wide. How's work?

MRS MORGAN: OK, thank you.

DENTIST: Yes, you need a couple of fillings.

MRS MORGAN: .Will . . . . you do them now?

DENTIST: Yes, if you like.

MRS MORGAN: (1) . . . . I have to have an injection?

> Score:
> 8

DENTIST: I'm not sure. You (2) . . . . need one. I (3) . . . . just have another look. Yes, I think you'd better have an injection. They're quite big fillings.

MRS MORGAN: (4) . . . . it hurt?

DENTIST: It depends. It (5) . . . . hurt a bit but you (6) . . . . be lucky.

MRS MORGAN: How long (7) . . . . it take to work?

DENTIST: Just a few seconds. There! Now you (8) . . . . feel the drill.

2 Look at the chart and write questions and answers about Granny Morgan's childhood using *used to*.

School: Went to Dover Elementary School.
1 *Home:* Lived in Harbour Street, Dover.
2 *Hobbies:* Liked knitting and reading.
3 *TV programmes:* Didn't watch TV. Listened to the radio.
4 *Holidays:* Went to the beach.
5 *Food:* A lot of roast meat and vegetables.

(Where) .Where. did.she. use. to. go. to. school.? . . . .

.She. used. to. go. to. Dover. Elementary. School. . . . .

1 (Where) . . . .

. . . .

2 (What) . . . .

. . . .

3 (Which) . . . .

. . . .

4 (Where) . . . .

. . . .

5 (What) . . . .

. . . .

Score:
10

3 Complete the crossword.

1 S Q U A R E (crossword grid with numbers 1–6)	1, 2, 3, 4, 5, 6 (pictures)

Score:
5

4 Write statements and responses: ✖✖ = can't stand, ✖ = hate, — = don't mind, ✔ = like.

✖✖ go/dentist

I can't stand going to the dentist. . . . .
No, nor can I. . . . .

✖ tidy/room

I hate tidying my room. . . . .
Yes, so do I. . . . .

1 ✖✖ do/washing up

. . . .
. . . .

2 ✔ visit/grandmother

. . . .
. . . .

3 — go/shopping

. . . .
. . . .

4 ✖ wear/hat

. . . .
. . . .

5 — make/bed

. . . .
. . . .

6 ✖✖ watch/football

. . . .

Score:
12

. . . .

5 Read the passage and answer the questions.

A hundred and fifty years ago, Britain was a very different place from the country it is today. Many people in Britain were very poor. They used to work long hours in factories and they didn't use to earn much money. Their children didn't use to go to school. They used to work in factories, too.

Most people walked to work because there were no trains, buses or cars. Only the rich travelled in their own carriages. People didn't use to have holidays very often because if they had a holiday, they weren't paid. Sometimes people couldn't find work and they died because they didn't have enough to eat. Life in Britain today is certainly a lot easier than it was in the nineteenth century.

Were most people in Britain rich 150 years ago?

. No, they weren't. . . . .

1 Where did many people use to work?

. . . .

2 Did poor children go to school?

. . . .

3 What did the children use to do?

. . . .

4 How did people travel if they didn't have money?

. . . .

5 How did they travel if they had money?

. . . .

Score:
5

6 Now write about life 150 years ago in your country or a country which you know about.

. . . .

. . . .

. . . .

. . . .

. . . .

. . . .

. . . .

. . . .

. . . .

Score:
10

Score:
50

Test 6 (Lessons 26-30)

1 Complete the sentences with the correct tense of the verb.

If you . . . *ask* . . . (ask) the teacher, she . . .*'ll explain* . . . . (explain) the exercise.

1 If you . . . . (go) by train, you . . . .(arrive) at 6 o'clock.

2 If he . . . . (see) the film, I'm sure he . . . . (like) it.

3 If she . . . . (not/study), she . . . . (fail) her exam.

4 If it . . . . (be) sunny tomorrow, we . . . . (go) to the beach.

5 If it . . . . (rain) tomorrow, we . . . . (stay) at home.

Score: 10

2 Write what Janet's trainer says.

Janet, you must train harder.

not / train harder
not / be / fit

If you don't train harder, you won't be fit. . . . . . .

. . . .

1 not / be / fit
   not / win / race

. . . .

. . . .

2 not / win /race
   not / get / medal

. . . .

. . . .

3 not / get / medal
   not / get into / school / team

. . . .

. . . .

Score: 6

3 Write the adverbs and the comparative adverbs.

Adjectives	Adverbs	Comparative adverbs
regular	.regularly.	.more regularly. . . . . . .
sensible	. . . .	. . . .
good	. . . .	. . . .
bad	. . . .	. . . .
slow	. . . .	. . . .

Adjectives	Adverbs	Comparative adverbs
early	....	....
fast	....	....
quick	....	....
hard	....	....

Score:

8

4 Read the text about Jupiter and label the diagram.

Jupiter is the largest planet in our solar system and is the fifth from the sun. It goes round the sun every twelve years and is 778 million kilometres away from it. Jupiter is mostly made up of hydrogen, helium and ammonia. This mixture of hydrogen and ammonia is probably what causes Jupiter's distinctive colouring. The colours change from day to day and include green, yellow, orange and brown. The planet often appears to be red, and it has a strange distinctive red spot on its surface. Scientists do not know exactly what causes this spot but they think it may be phosphorus.

Jupiter has at least fifteen moons. Four of them, Io, Europa, Ganymede and Callisto are brighter than the others, and are called 'Galilean Satellites' because the scientist Galileo discovered them.

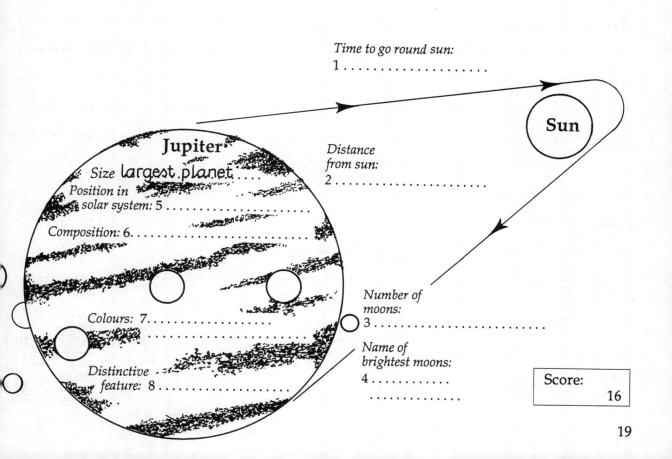

Time to go round sun:
1 ....

Sun

Jupiter

Size largest planet....

Position in solar system: 5 ....

Composition: 6. ....

Distance from sun:
2 ....

Colours: 7.......................
....

Number of moons:
3 ....

Distinctive feature: 8 ....

Name of brightest moons:
4 ....
....

Score:

16

19

5 Now look at the information below about the planet Saturn and write about it.

Time to go round sun: 29.5 years

Sun

Distance from sun: 1,400 million km

Saturn

Size: second largest planet in solar system

Position: sixth in solar system

Composition: hydrogen and helium

Colours: white yellow and orange

Distinctive feature: five beautiful 'rings' made of small pieces of rock and ice

Number of moons: 10

....

....

....

....

....

....

....

....

....

Score: 10

Score: 50

Test 7 (Lessons 31-35)

1 Look at the list of jobs and write what people have got to do for the school play.

Anne - bring the records

John - set up the disco equipment

Sue - put up the lights

Kate and Andy - fix the microphone and speakers

Alan and Rob - make the sandwiches

Miss Harris - buy the drinks

. Anne's got to bring the records. . . . .

1 . . . .

2 . . . .

3 . . . .

4 . . . .

5 . . . .

Score: 5

2 Complete the conversation about the party plans.

CAROLE: Shall I bring the records for Anne?

MISS HARRIS: . . Thanks, but Anne should bring them herself. . . . .

CAROLE: Well, shall I set up the disco equipment for John?

MISS HARRIS: (1) . . . .

CAROLE: Perhaps I should put the lights up for Sue.

MISS HARRIS: (2) . . . .

CAROLE: I'll help Kate and Andy to fix the microphone.

MISS HARRIS: (3) . . . .

CAROLE: I can make the sandwiches for Alan and Rob.

MISS HARRIS: (4) . . . .

CAROLE: Well, shall I buy the drinks for you?

MISS HARRIS: (5) . . . .

CAROLE: Well, what shall I do then?

MISS HARRIS: Just come and enjoy yourself!

Score: 5

3 Look at the notes about Mr Green and write questions and answers, using *for* or *since*.

Live in Dover: 8 years
Work at Castle School: 6 years
Teach Andy: 3 years
Play football: 1969
Collect stamps: 1 year
Drive a Fiat: January

How long has he been living in Dover? . . . .

He's been living in Dover for eight years . . . .

1 . . . .

. . . .

2 . . . .

. . . .

3 . . . .

. . . .

4 . . . .

. . . .

5 . . . .

. . . .

Score:
10

4 Write what the people said in class yesterday.

Alan (I can't see the board.)   3 Kate (I think it's very boring.)

1 Robert (I can't understand the question.)   4 John (I hope the exam is easy.)

2 Sue (I know I can do question six.)   5 Tim (I don't like Geography!)

(say) . Alan said (that) he couldn't see the board . . . .

1 (say) . . . .

2 (know) . . . .

3 (think) . . . .

4 (hope) . . . .

5 (say) . . . .

Score:
10

5 Complete the passage.

Scotland is a country . . which . . is situated in the north (1) . . . . Britain. Among the first inhabitants of Scotland were the Celts, (2) . . . . arrived there from other parts of Europe. The Celts and their descendents spread throughout Scotland, both (3) . . . . the mountains and in the lowland. Many of them lived (4) . . . . the coasts and (5) . . . . the "lochs" (lakes). They fished (6) . . . . the sea and the lochs, they hunted, and they also cultivated the land on their "crofts" (small farms). People lived like this for many hundreds of years.

In recent years, this traditional way of life has changed a lot. Nowadays, most people (7) . . . . live in Scotland work (8) . . . . offices or in factories. Very few people work (9) . . . . crofts and the fishing industry is much smaller (10) . . . . it used to be.

Score:
10

6 Now write about your own country or a country which you know.

. . . .

Score:
10

Score:
50

23

Test 8 (Lessons 36-40)

1 Read this information about the agriculture and industry of a country and then write a speech about it in the passive.

They grow apples in the north. They grow grapes throughout the country and they produce some very good wine. They produce orange juice in the south. They make cars and buses in factories in the centre of the country. They sell the cars to many countries in Europe, and also to America. However, they don't export the buses. They use them in the country itself.

Score: 7

66 ...... Apples are grown in the north of the country. ....

....

....

....

....

....

.... **99**

....

2 Look at the crossword and then complete the clues using *made of* or *made from*.

DOWN

1 This is made of glass............
..We look through it...............

3 ....
.We put it on our bread............

ACROSS

2 ....
.We wear it.............................

3 ....
.We study from it.....................

4 ....
We eat it................................

5 ....
We look at ourselves in it.............

		¹W					³B	O	O	K
²S	H	I	R	T			B			
		N					U			
		D					T			
		⁴O	M	E	L	E	T	T	E	
		W					E			
			⁵M	I	R	R	O	R		

Score: 5

3 Rewrite the sentences using the past perfect.

The train left. Then Sue got to the station.

.When Sue got to the station, the train had left...............

1 Everybody went home. Then John arrived at the party.

. . . .

2 The cat ate Robert's dinner. Then Robert came into the room.

. . . .

3 Somebody stole Kate and Andy's suitcase. Then Kate and Andy came back.

. . . .

4 Sarah went out. Then Mary phoned her.

. . . .

5 Somebody took Janet's purse. Then Janet looked in her handbag.

. . . .

4 Write the words.

Score: 10

sacsetiu .. suitcase.....   1 reappsnew ....   2 nin ....

3 yeradvrag ....   4 heros ....   5 leggrusm ....

5 Complete the sentences with *who, which* or *where*.

Score: 5

He's the teacher ....who.... taught me English.

1 This is the shop .... they sell nice icecream.

2 I like videos .... have strange settings.

3 That's the guitarist .... had a hit record.

4 My brother's a person .... can't stand going to the dentist.

5 That's the house .... I was born.

6 London's a city .... has a lot of tourists.

7 He's a singer .... writes his own songs.

8 Here's a place .... we can sit down.

Score: 8

6 Read the passage and answer the questions.

John's favourite video at the moment is a conceptual video. The music is played in a very exotic setting - a smuggler's cave. When the video starts, it is dark. Then the lead singer walks into the cave, holding a candle in front of him. The rest of the performers follow him and they start to play. All the performers wear smugglers' costumes with big, gold earrings and eyepatches. Around them in the cave are boxes and barrels where the smuggled goods are stored.

After they have played for about three minutes, the lead singer blows out the candle and the "smugglers" get on a boat which is waiting outside the cave.

Is John's favourite video a performance video?

. No, it isn't. It's a conceptual video. .

1 Where is the music played?

. . . .

2 What does the lead singer hold?

. . . .

3 What do the performers wear?

. . . .

. . . .

4 Where are the smuggled goods stored?

. . . .

. . . .

5 Where do the performers go at the end?

. . . .

Score: 5

7 Now write about your favourite film or video.

. . . .

. . . .

. . . .

. . . .

. . . .

. . . .

. . . .

Score: 10

. . . .

Score: 50

Test 9 (Lessons 41- 45)

1 Complete the conversation.

TEACHER: Kate, have you seen John? I want him . **to. collect**. . (collect) the homework for me.

KATE: He (1) . . . . (not/arrive) yet, sir. Perhaps he's had a puncture.

TEACHER: This isn't the first time he (2) . . . . (be) late.

You (3) . . . . (better/collect) the homework instead.

KATE: Yes, sir. Oh, look, he (4) . . . . (just/arrive).

JOHN: I'm sorry I'm late, sir. The traffic (5) . . . . (be) terrible this morning.

TEACHER: Well, you (6) . . . . (better/not/be) late again. If you

(7) . . . . (not/arrive) earlier in future, you

(8) . . . . (have to stay) after school and do some extra work!

Score:
8

2 Look at the pictures and complete the sentences with *might, could, must* or *can't*.

He . . **could**. . . be at an airport.

1 He . . . . be at a railway station.

2 There . . . . be a skeleton inside the suitcase because we can see it.

3 It . . . . be his suitcase because he looks too surprised.

4 It . . . . be the day time because he's holding a candle.

5 He . . . . be in a graveyard because we can see some graves.

6 He . . . . be a smuggler or a pirate.

Score:
6

3 Match the words with the correct dictionary definition.

watch   ☑ ②

see   ☐

look for   ☐

look at   ☐

stare at   ☐

1 +*v-ing*] to use the eyes; have or use the power of sight: *It was so dark he could hardly* ▆▆▆▆. |*He doesn't* ▆▆▆ *well in his right eye.* **2** [T +*(that)*; not be +*v-ing*] to get sight of; notice, examine, or recognize by looking: *I looked for her but I couldn't* ▆▆ *her in the crowd.*|

2 *v* **1** [I;T] to look at (some activity or event): *Do you often* ▆▆▆ *television?*|*They* ▆▆▆ *the car go past.*

4 ▆▆▆▆ [T] **1** to watch: ▆▆▆▆ *the traffic going past the window* **2** to regard; judge: *He* ▆▆▆ *work in a different way now he's in charge.*

3 ▆▆▆▆ to look fixedly (at) with wide-open eyes, as in wonder, fear, anger, or deep thought: *It's rude to* ▆▆▆▆▆▆▆▆

5 *v prep* [T] to try to find

Score: 4

4 Write questions and answers in the passive about these facts.

Bartholdi designed the Statue of Liberty in 1877.

1 Alexander Graham Bell invented the telephone in 1874.

2 The Wright brothers built the first aeroplane with an engine in 1903.

3 Columbus discovered America in 1492.

4 Some pilots discovered the Nazca lines in 1939.

5 Galileo discovered the mountains on the Moon in 1610.

6 Sir William Herschel discovered the planet of Uranus in 1781.

When was the Statue of Liberty designed? ....

It was designed in 1877. ....

1 ....

....

2 ....

....

3 ....

....

4 ....

....

5 ....

....

6 ....

....

Score: 12

5 Read the passage and answer the questions.

On 18th December 1751 a Dutch ship called the "Geldermalsen" left the port of Canton in China to go to Europe. The ship was carrying tea, silk and fine porcelain (cups, saucers, plates and bowls). The porcelain was packed in the tea to stop it breaking. On the way to Europe, the ship hit some rocks in the South China Sea, and it sank on 3rdJanuary 1752.

There the wreck stayed, at the bottom of the sea, until it was discovered by Captain Michael Hatcher in 1985. The tea and silk had disappeared but the porcelain was still there.

It was brought to the surface by Captain Hatcher and a team of divers. A lot of it was in perfect condition. It was taken to Amsterdam and cleaned and then it was sold, in April 1986. People came from all over the world to buy the blue and white cups, saucers, plates and bowls, which are beautifully decorated with pictures of flowers, trees and fish. They are a truly wonderful example of Chinese porcelain of the eighteenth century.

Where was the "Geldermalsen" going? ..*It was going to Europe*......

1 What was the ship carrying?......

2 How was the porcelain packed?......

3 What happened to the ship in 1752?......

4 When was the wreck disovered?......

5 Were the tea and silk still there?......

6 What did the divers do?......

7 Where was the porcelain taken?......

8 What happened to it in 1986?......

9 What do the cups and saucers look like?......

10 Why did people buy them?......

Score: 10

6 Now write about *either* the Nazca lines *or* another discovery which interests you.

......

......

......

......

......

......

Score: 10

Score: 50

Test 10 (Lessons 46-50)

1 Read the text about Debbie then write her wishes.

Debbie thinks that her hair is too curly and it's the wrong colour. It's blonde and she would like dark hair. She also thinks that she's too tall and would like to be shorter. She can't swim or speak French but she wants to. She hasn't got a dog but she would like one. She lives in a city but she would prefer to live in the country.

(curly hair) . *Debbie wishes she hadn't got curly hair.* . . . .

1 (blonde hair) . . . .

2 (dark hair) . . . .

3 (tall) . . . .

4 (shorter) . . . .

5 (swim) . . . .

6 (speak French) . . . .

7 (dog) . . . .

8 (country) . . . .

Score:
8

2 Complete the sentences with the correct form of the verb.

If I . . . . . . *had* . . . . (have) a lot of money, I . . . . *would buy* . . . . . (buy) a new bike.

1 If he . . . . (study) harder, he . . . . (pass) his exams.

2 If they . . . . (tell) their mother, perhaps she . . . .

   (can/help)

3 I . . . . (not/eat) so many sweets if I . . . . (be) you.

4 You . . . . (be) healthier if you . . . . (give up) smoking.

5 They . . . . (come) to see us if they . . . . (have) a car.

6 If I . . . . (be) you, I . . . . (take) an aspirin.

7 If you . . . . (join) a club, you . . . . (make) new friends.

Score:
14

30

3 Write questions.

What / do / win / a million pounds

.What would you do if you won a million pounds?. . . . . I'd buy a boat.

1 What / eat / be / too fat

. . . . I'd eat vegetables and salad.

2 Where / go/ have /car

. . . . I'd drive to France.

3 Who / invite / have / big / party

. . . . I'd invite all my friends.

4 Where / live / be / shipwrecked / on / desert / island

. . . . I'd build a shelter from palm leaves.

5 What / drink / be / on / desert island

. . . . I'd drink coconut milk.

6 What / wear / visit / Queen

. . . . I'd wear my best suit.

Score:

6

4 Complete the text with the correct preposition or adverb.

John Adams lived . . by . . himself (1) . . . . an old house (2) . . . . the mouth of a river,

where he photographed animals. John was a hunchback. (3) . . . . . . first the village people

were afraid (4) . . . . . . him but they soon got used (5) . . . . . . him. However, no one found

(6) . . . . . . that John was a kind man who loved animals.

Score:

6

**5 Read Kevin's letter
to a magazine problem page
and answer the questions.**

Dear Street Beat,

My problem is that I like a girl who probably doesn't like me. I met her at a school disco and I danced with her once, but when I asked her to dance again, she said no. She lives in the same street as me so I see her on the school bus every day. She thinks that I am following her around but I'm not really. I wish that I could talk to her but every time I try she walks away. If I were tall, dark and handsome, perhaps she would like me better. Do you think I should change my hairstyle or buy some new clothes? Please tell me what you think.

Kevin, Dover

What's Kevin's problem? .. He likes a girl who probably doesn't like him. ....

1 Where did he meet her? ....

2 Why does he see her on the school bus? ....

3 Is he following her? ....

4 What does he want to do? ....

5 Does he think that he is good-looking? ....

6 How does he think that he could solve the problem? ....

Score:
6

**6 Now *either* write a letter to Kevin giving him advice *or* write a conversation with Kevin
in which you give him advice.**

....

....

....

....

....

....

....

Score:
10

Score:
50